LIFE PROCESSES

Life Cycles

Holly Wallace

Heinemann
LIBRARY

www.heinemann.co.uk
Visit our website to find out more information about Heinemann Library books.

To order:
 Phone 44 (0) 1865 888066
Send a fax to 44 (0) 1865 314091
 Visit the Heinemann Bookshop at www.heinemann.co.uk to browse our catalogue and order online.

First published in Great Britain by Heinemann Library,
Halley Court, Jordan Hill, Oxford OX2 8EJ
a division of Reed Educational and Professional Publishing Ltd.
Heinemann is a registered trademark of Reed Educational & Professional Publishing Ltd.

OXFORD MELBOURNE AUCKLAND
JOHANNESBURG BLANTYRE GABORONE
IBADAN PORTSMOUTH (NH) USA CHICAGO

Designed by Celia Floyd
Originated by Dot Gradations
Printed by Wing King Tong, in Hong Kong

ISBN 0 431 10885 4 (hardback)
04 03 02 01
10 9 8 7 6 5 4 3 2

ISBN 0 431 10892 7 (paperback)
04 03 02 01
10 9 8 7 6 5 4 3 2 1

British Library Cataloguing in Publication Data

Wallace, Holly
  Life cycles. – (Life processes)
  1. Life cycles (Biology) – Juvenile literature
  I. Title
  571.8

Acknowledgements

The Publishers would like to thank the following for permission to reproduce photographs:

Corbis: pg.24; *NHPA*: MI Walker pg.4, GI Bernard pg.5, pg.7, pg.13, ANT pg.5, Brian Hawkes pg.8, Stephen Dalton pg.12, pg.13, pg.19, NA Callow pg.13, Ron Fotheringham pg.13, Stephen Krasemann pg.14, pg.15, Pavel German pg.21, Yves Lanceau pg.26, Gerard Lacz pg.27; *Oxford Scientific Films*: Colin Milkins pg.15, Mark Deeble & Victoria Stone pg.16, Zig Leszczynski pg.20, Doug Allan pg.22, Daniel J Cox pg.23; *Planet Earth Pictures*: Doug Perrine pg.16; *Robert Harding Picture Library*: Raj Kamal pg.11.

Cover photograph reproduced with permission of Oxford Scientific Films.

Every effort has been made to contact copyright holders of any material reproduced in this book. Any omissions will be rectified in subsequent printings if notice is given to the Publisher.

Any words appearing in the text in bold, **like this**, are explained in the glossary.

Contents

Introduction

The six books in this series explore the features and life processes that keep animals and plants alive. *Life Cycles* looks at the different stages in a living thing's life, from its birth to the way it grows and develops. It also describes how living things look after their young, and we find some suprisingly caring parents. All living things eventually die, and so living things reproduce to replace those that die. Then the amazing cycle of life can begin again.

Living and dying

A life cycle describes the main stages in a living thing's life, such as birth, growth, reproduction and death. 'Reproduction' means the creation of new life. All living things reproduce in order to continue their **species** and to replace those that die. They reproduce in two main ways, which are called **asexual** reproduction and **sexual** reproduction.

Asexual reproduction

Asexual reproduction is the simplest form of reproduction. It happens in many simple animals and plants. It is called asexual because it does not involve sex. In asexual reproduction, only one parent is needed. There are different types of asexual reproduction. The parent may simply split in two, or part of the parent may bud or split off to form a new individual. This new individual is always identical to its parent because it shares the same **genetic** make-up.

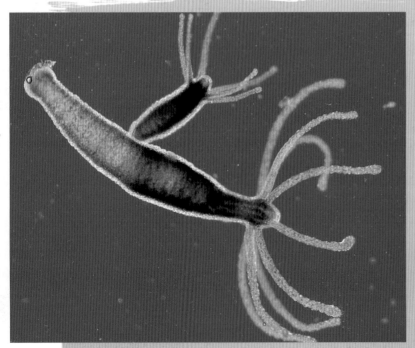

A hydra reproducing asexually by budding.

Hydra reproduction

Asexual reproduction is more common in plants than in animals, but some animals do reproduce this way. A hydra is a tiny, tentacled creature that lives in freshwater ponds. It can reproduce by 'budding'. A group of cells grows on the hydra's stalk-like body, produces tentacles, then buds off its parent to form a new animal.

Sexual reproduction

All flowering plants and most animals reproduce sexually. There are always two parents in sexual reproduction. Each makes sex cells called male and female **gametes**, and each carries half of the genetic material for the new individual. The two must join, or fuse, together, to create a **zygote**, or new cell. This process is called **fertilization**. From the fertilized cell, a new living thing will develop.

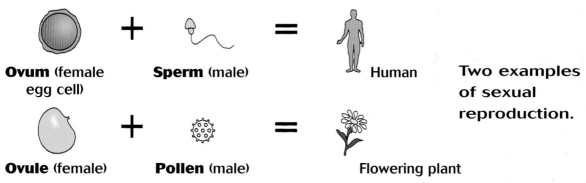

Ovum (female egg cell) + **Sperm** (male) = Human

Ovule (female) + **Pollen** (male) = Flowering plant

Two examples of sexual reproduction.

Strawberry plants reproduce sexually with seeds and asexually by putting out side stems called runners which put down roots and grow into new plants.

Internal and external fertilization

In some animals, fertilization takes place inside the female's body. In others, fertilization is external. Crabs belong to a group of animals called crustaceans. The female crab sheds her egg cells in the sand on the shore or in shallow water. The male then fertilizes them with his sperm. The fertilized eggs are washed out to sea where they hatch into **larvae**.

A female crab releasing her eggs into the sea, ready for the male to fertilize.

Flowering plants

Flowering plants reproduce by **sexual** reproduction. A plant's flowers contain the plant's male and female reproductive organs. New plants grow from seeds. For a seed to be produced, **pollen** needs to be transferred from the male parts of the plant to the female parts. This is called **pollination**. Some plants self-pollinate, which means that they use their own supply of pollen. However, most cross-pollinate, which means that they need pollen from another plant to make their seeds. When pollination has happened, the flower dies.

Inside a buttercup flower

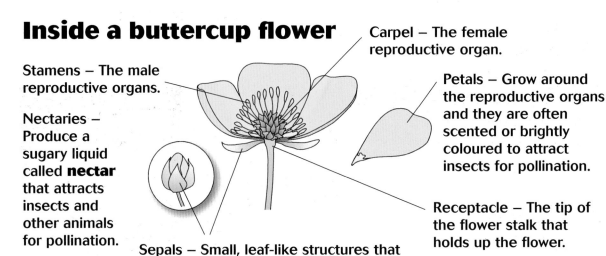

Carpel – The female reproductive organ.

Stamens – The male reproductive organs.

Nectaries – Produce a sugary liquid called **nectar** that attracts insects and other animals for pollination.

Petals – Grow around the reproductive organs and they are often scented or brightly coloured to attract insects for pollination.

Receptacle – The tip of the flower stalk that holds up the flower.

Sepals – Small, leaf-like structures that protect the flower while it is still in bud.

The carpel is made up of an ovary, a stigma and a style. The ovary contains tiny **ovules**, the female sex cells. The stigma catches the pollen grains. The style joins the stigma to the ovary.

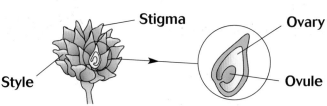

Stigma

Ovary

Style

Ovule

A stamen is made up of a filament and an anther. The anther produces pollen grains, the male sex cells. The filament holds the anther up for pollination.

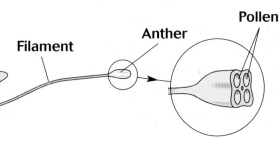

Filament

Anther

Pollen

Pollen transfer

For a seed to grow, pollen must be transferred from the male to the female parts of a flower. The anther splits open, releasing millions of tiny pollen grains. Once a grain lands on the female stigma, it grows a long tube that reaches down the style and into the ovary. The pollen grain has two **nuclei**. One fuses with the nucleus of the egg cell inside the ovule to form a new cell. The other fuses with two other cells in the ovule to form a store of food.

Did you know?

Different plants have different life-spans. Some flowering plants only live for a year. They grow, produce their flowers and seeds very quickly, then die. They are called **annuals**. Some live for many years but die down at the end of each growing season, growing new shoots at the start of the next. They are called **perennials**.

Flower designs

Flowers rely on the wind and animals, such as insects, birds and bats, to transfer their pollen. A flower's shape, colour and smell show how it is pollinated. Wind-pollinated flowers, such as grass flowers, are small and drab because they do not need to attract pollinating animals. Insect-pollinated flowers have bright petals, sweet smells and a store of sugary nectar to tempt butterflies and bees. The insects visit the flowers to drink their nectar and become coated in pollen which they carry to the next flower they visit.

A honeybee visiting a flower.

From seeds to plants

Once the **pollen** has **fertilized** the **ovule**, the ovule grows into a seed. It contains the beginnings of a new plant and a store of food for the plant to use until it grows leaves and can make food for itself. The ovary develops into a protective fruit around the seed. The fruit may be a nut, berry or pod. The seed must travel away from the parent plant to avoid competition for light and space and find a suitable place to grow. The process by which a seed produces its first root and shoot, and begins to grow into a new plant is called **germination**.

The main parts of a seed are shown here.

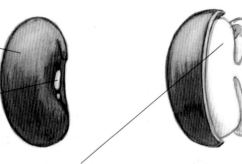

Testa – The protective casing around the seed.

Hilum – The scar on the seed, showing where the ovule was attached to the ovary.

Plumule – The plant's first shoot.

Radicle – The plant's first root.

Cotyledon or seed leaf – Food for the new plant is stored in the cotyledons. Some seeds have two cotyledons (dicotyledons, such as daisies and poppies). Others have one (monocotyledons, such as daffodils and grasses).

Seed dispersal

Many plants rely on wind, water, birds and animals to disperse their seeds. Dandelion seeds are very light and attached to tiny, fluffy parachutes. They are easily blown away by the wind. Birds eat fleshy fruits, such as berries or rosehips. The seeds or pips pass through their bodies and are dispersed with their droppings. Burdock fruits are covered in tiny hooks that catch on to animals' wool or fur.

This diagram shows how a seed germinates.

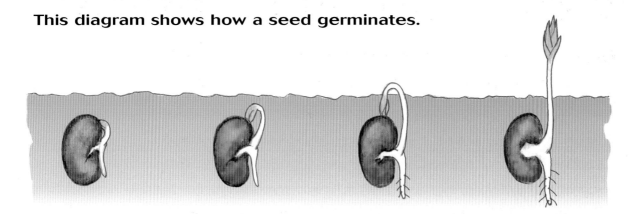

1. The seed takes in water and swells up. Chemicals inside the seed convert the starchy food store into **glucose**, which the seed needs for growth.

2. A few days later, the radicle pushes through the testa into the soil. Root hairs absorb water and minerals from the soil.

3. The plumule grows upwards through the soil. It is hooked so it can push through the soil without damaging the growing tip.

4. Soon the plant grows its first leaves and begins to make food by **photosynthesis**.

Conifer life cycles

Conifers have cones instead of flowers or fruit. Each cone is either male or female. Male pollen cells are carried to female cones to fertilize the female cells and produce seeds. The seeds are protected inside the cones, which harden and turn brown. When the weather is warm and dry, the cones open up and release the seeds. The seeds have tiny wings for floating on the breeze.

Bristlecone pine cones.

Growing from spores

Some plants do not reproduce from seeds. They produce microscopic, dust-like specks of living material, called **spores**. Millions of spores are released into the air and carried away by the wind. If they find a suitable place to grow, they will develop into new plants. Plants that reproduce with spores include ferns, mosses, horsetails and liverworts. **Fungi** also reproduce with spores.

Fern life cycles

Ferns produce spores on the undersides of their **fronds**, in structures called **sporangia**. These are arranged in groups and often look like tiny patches of rust. When the spores are ripe, the sporangia open and release them into the air. Even if a spore lands in a good spot, it does not grow directly into a new fern. Ferns have two stages to their life cycles. The first is **asexual**, and the second is **sexual**.

The life cycle of a fern.

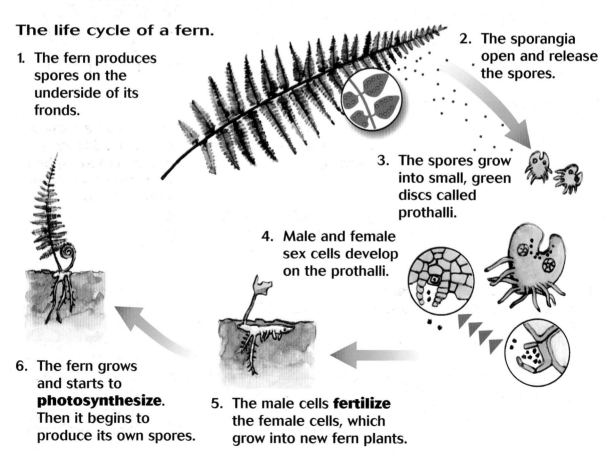

1. The fern produces spores on the underside of its fronds.

2. The sporangia open and release the spores.

3. The spores grow into small, green discs called prothalli.

4. Male and female sex cells develop on the prothalli.

5. The male cells **fertilize** the female cells, which grow into new fern plants.

6. The fern grows and starts to **photosynthesize**. Then it begins to produce its own spores.

10

How fungi reproduce

Fungi do not have flowers, leaves, proper roots or stems. They do not have **chlorophyll** and cannot photosynthesize. Fungi used to be classified as plants but they now form their own, separate **kingdom**. Like ferns, fungi reproduce with spores. In mushrooms and toadstools, these grow under the cap, on ridges called **gills**. The cap protects the gills from rain while the stalk holds them up so that they can fall easily and catch the breeze.

Did you know?

Fungi produce huge numbers of spores. Giant puffballs can measure up to 120 centimetres across, but more usually they measure about the same as a large melon. They can produce an incredible 70,000,000,000,000 spores, which they 'puff' out in thick clouds. Puffballs do not have gills but burst open to release their spores.

A giant puffball releasing spores.

How a toadstool grows.

1. A spore lands on the ground and starts to **germinate**.

2. It grows into a mass of underground feeding threads, called hyphae, which form a structure called a 'button'.

3. The button grows upwards. Its outer skin splits to show a stalk and a cap.

4. The stalk grows taller and the cap expands to uncover its gills. The gills begin to produce spores. The whole process may only take a few hours.

Insect life cycles

Most insects hatch from eggs laid by the female. Only a very few types, such as aphids, produce live young. Most insects go through amazing series of changes as they develop from eggs into adults. This is called **metamorphosis**. An adult insect's life may be very short. An adult mayfly, for example, only lives for one day. But during that time, the insect must find a mate. After mating, the female lays her eggs, often on plant leaves or stems for the young to feed on.

Complete metamorphosis

Some insects, such as moths, butterflies, bees and beetles, go through complete metamorphosis. The newly-hatched young look very different from the adults. They change from eggs into **larvae**, then into **pupae**, before emerging as adults. On the opposite page you can follow the metamorphosis of a large white butterfly.

Incomplete metamorphosis

Some insects, such as locusts, grasshoppers and dragonflies, go through incomplete metamorphosis. The young look similar to adults. They develop from eggs into **nymphs**, then into adults. Here you can follow the metamorphosis of a desert locust.

Locust life cycle.

1. The locust lays her eggs in the sand. They take about ten days to hatch.

2. The eggs hatch into young called nymphs. These look like adult locusts except that they do not have wings.

3. The nymphs feed and grow. Like all insects, locusts have to shed, or **moult**, their hard, outer skins in order to grow. Locusts do this five times as they grow up.

4. During the fifth moult (pictured), an adult locust emerges, complete with wings.

Butterfly life cycle.

1. A female large white butterfly lays her barrel-shaped eggs on a cabbage leaf. They take about a week to hatch.

2. The eggs hatch into caterpillars (butterfly larvae). They spend their time feeding on the cabbage leaves and growing.

3. Each caterpillar spins a silk **chrysalis** around its body and hangs underneath a cabbage leaf. It becomes a pupa inside the chrysalis and starts to metamorphose.

4. Inside the chrysalis, the pupa caterpillar's body is broken down. New organs and tissue grow to form an adult butterfly.

5. About three weeks later, the chrysalis splits open and an adult butterfly struggles out. Blood flows into its soft wings, making them rigid and ready for flight.

Did you know?

Most female insects lay their eggs and then abandon them, but female earwigs are caring mothers. They lay their eggs in a hole in the ground and stand guard over them. They wash them often to keep them free from **parasites**. Even when the eggs hatch, the mothers protect the young until they can look after themselves.

Spiders and scorpions

Spiders and scorpions belong to a group of animals called **arachnids**. Like insects, their young hatch from eggs. The eggs are **fertilized** inside the mother's body. When the young, or **nymphs**, hatch, they look like miniature versions of their parents. Then they **moult** several times before they reach adult size. Ticks and mites are also arachnids. Adult arachnids have eight legs. Newly-hatched ticks and mites only have six. They develop two more legs as they moult and grow. Arachnid lifespans range from a few weeks in some types of mite to 30 years in some large spiders.

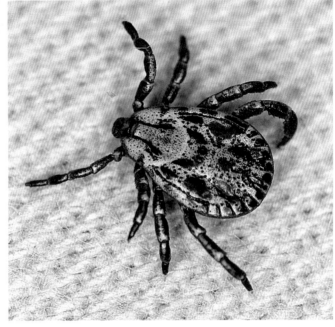

A rocky mountain tick is an arachnid.

Dancing scorpions

Before they mate, some scorpions perform an elaborate courtship dance. First the male waves his pincers in the air, taps his feet on the ground and shakes his body to attract a female. Then the male and female link pincers and 'dance' to and fro, for hours on end. The eggs are fertilized inside the female's body.

Scorpions and young

After fertilization, the female scorpion lays up to 95 eggs. The eggs hatch almost at once. Then the baby scorpions climb up their mother's pincers and on to her back. They cling on with their tiny legs and sharp pincers. Their mother carries them about, out of reach of enemies, until they have moulted for the first time and are able to fend for themselves.

Spider eggs

Because so many spiders' eggs die or are eaten, many kinds of spiders produce huge numbers of eggs to make sure that some survive. Cave spiders lay a single egg, but other spiders lay up to 2500 at a time. The eggs are protected in a silk sac, or purse. Some kinds of spider guard and protect their eggs, others leave them alone.

Spider care

After mating, the female wolf spider spins a silk purse around her eggs. The case remains attached to her spinnerets (the silk-producing glands on her **abdomen**). When she goes out hunting, she drags the purse with her. When the baby spiders hatch, she carries them on her back until they are able to look after themselves.

A female wolf spider carrying her young on her back.

Did you know?

Horseshoe crabs are not crabs at all but close relations of arachnids. They are found in warm seas. The crabs spend most of their lives on the ocean bed, searching for worms and clams to eat. But every spring, at high tide, hundreds of thousands gather on the shore to mate and lay their eggs in the sand. The young are only 2 centimetres long when they hatch. They have a risky dash to the sea and many are eaten by birds.

Horseshoe crabs laying their eggs on the beach at high tide.

Fish life cycles

Most fish lay their eggs, or **spawn**, in the sea, and in rivers and lakes. In many fish, **fertilization** takes place externally, outside the female's body. The female lays her eggs in the water, then the male covers them with his **sperm**. Some fish lay huge numbers of eggs. For example, a cod may lay six million eggs that float to the surface. Because the eggs contain a supply of food for the growing baby, they are also a nourishing source of food for birds and other fish, and many are eaten. Others are not fertilized. Laying a large number of eggs is a way of making sure that some, at least, survive. Other fish, including some sharks, give birth to live young.

A live lemon shark being born.

Did you know?

Most female fish lay their eggs, then leave them unattended. But some cichlid fish, known as 'mouthbrooders', take great care to protect their young. The eggs are fertilized, then the females keep them in their mouth for ten days or so until they hatch. Even then, the young fish stay close to their mothers and swim back into their mouth if danger threatens.

An emperor cichlid with its young.

Salmon life cycle

Most fish spend their whole lives either in the sea or in freshwater. Salmon spend time in both. A salmon hatches and dies in the same stretch of fast-flowing river. But, in between, it makes an extraordinary journey out to sea to feed and grow into an adult. Here you can follow the sockeye salmon's life cycle.

Flatfish features

When young, a flatfish, such as a sole or a plaice, is the same shape as most ordinary fish. But a few weeks after it hatches, it begins to change shape. One eye moves round to the other side of its head so that both eyes are on the same side. After about six weeks, its body is completely flat. It sinks to the seabed to lie on its blind side. Here it is perfectly camouflaged among the stones and sand.

1. The female salmon lays up to 5000 eggs in a river. They are fertilized by several males.

2. The eggs hatch into tiny fish called alevins. They carry a pouch of food that will last for several weeks.

3. The alevins grow into fry. The fry grow into smolts.

6. After spawning, the adults die and the life cycle begins again.

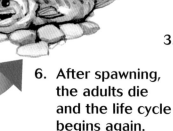

4. After spending between one and five years in freshwater, the smolts swim out to sea to feed and grow. They travel thousands of kilometres in a journey lasting for several years.

5. The adult salmon spend about four years at sea, then they return to the river of their birth to breed. They swim up-river and lay their eggs.

Amphibian life cycles

Amphibians are animals such as frogs, toads, newts and salamanders that are born in water, but as adults spend most of their lives on land. They return to the water to lay their eggs. Their name comes from the Greek word *amphibios* and means 'having two lives'. At first, their young are adapted to life in water. They breathe through **gills**, like fish, and have tails for swimming. Later, they develop features such as lungs and legs to help them survive on land. Like the changes that happen to growing insects, these changes are called **metamorphosis**.

Frog life cycle

Here you can follow the life cycle of a typical frog.

1. In spring, adult frogs arrive at a pond. The males croak loudly to attract a female.

2. As the frogs mate, the female lays over 2000 eggs which are **fertilized** by the male. The eggs, or **spawn**, are covered in jelly for protection. They float near the surface of the pond.

3. About two weeks later, the eggs hatch into tiny tadpoles that breathe through gills, taking in oxygen from the water.

5. The froglets spend more and more of their time out of the water, then leave the pond completely. It takes three years for them to be fully grown. In the wild, frogs have many enemies and their lives may be short. In captivity, however, they may live for up to ten years.

4. Over the next three months, the tadpoles develop lungs and legs. Their tails shrink and they look like tiny frogs.

Caring parents

Some amphibians look after their eggs very carefully. Male midwife toads wind strings of eggs around their back legs and carry them around with them. When the eggs are ready to hatch, the male goes to the pond and lowers his back legs into the water so that the tadpoles can swim away. The male Darwin's frog swallows his tadpoles and carries them in his throat. When they grow into froglets, he spits them out!

Breeding in water

In spring, frogs and toads go to a pond or lake to breed. Many return to the same breeding site year after year, often the same pond they were born in. They may travel several kilometres to reach their home pond, crossing dangerous roads and railways. They seem to use landmarks to find their way, and their sense of smell. But they may also be guided by the Earth's magnetic field.

Did you know?

The odd-looking axolotl is a species of salamander from Mexico. Like other salamanders, axolotls start life as tadpoles, or **larvae**, with feathery gills. Scientists have discovered that axolotls need the chemical, **iodine**, to complete their life cycles and turn into adults. Unfortunately, there is no iodine in their natural **habitat**. This means that the axolotls never mature, although they become **fertile** and are able to reproduce while still larvae.

A Mexican axolotl.

Reptile life cycles

Unlike **amphibians**, **reptiles** – such as snakes, turtles, crocodiles and lizards – lay their eggs on land. Their eggs have thick shells to stop them drying out. Inside the eggs is everything the young reptiles need to develop, including food, water and oxygen. Lizards and snakes lay eggs with flexible, leathery shells. Crocodiles lay eggs with hard shells. Some reptiles, especially those that live in cooler places, produce live young. Otherwise, the eggs might become too cold and the young inside die. Many reptiles lay their eggs in nests, dug in the sand or soil, or built of leaves and stems.

Snake life cycle

These are the main stages in the life cycle of an American corn snake (which you can see in the picture).

1. The female lays her eggs in a rotten tree stump.
2. Inside its egg, the young snake feeds on the **yolk** and grows. It spends about eight weeks **incubating**.
3. The snake cuts a slit in the eggshell, using its egg-tooth (the sharp piece of bone on its snout).
4. It spends the day in its shell, poking its head in and out.
5. Next day, it slithers out of the egg through another hole and off into the wild.
6. A few days later, it **moults** its skin for the first time to allow it to grow. It will do this several more times until it reaches adult size.

A corn snake coiled protectively around its eggs.

Crocodiles are caring parents. The female lays her eggs in a hole near the water's edge. She covers it with plants and soil to hide it from **predators**. She guards the nest for about three months, until the eggs hatch. When she hears a squeaking noise coming from the eggs, she knows it is time to dig them up. The baby crocodiles use their egg-teeth to break out of their shells. Then their mother picks them up in her mouth and carries them to the water. The babies stay close to their mother until they are about two years old.

Dash to the sea

Sea turtles spend most of their lives in the ocean, but the females come ashore to lay their eggs. Some sea turtles swim thousands of kilometres from their feeding grounds to their nesting sites. They mate off-shore, then the females dig a hole in the sand, lay their eggs and return to the sea. The newly-hatched turtles dig themselves out of the sand, then face a dangerous journey to the sea. Many are eaten by crabs and predatory birds.

A newly-hatched green turtle heads for the safety of the sea.

Did you know?

Reptiles are long-lived animals. Small snakes may live for up to twelve years and larger snakes for 40 years or longer. But the longest-lived reptile, and the longest-lived of any land animal, is the huge Marion's tortoise. A male Marion's tortoise was believed to be more than 152 years old when it was killed, accidentally, in 1918.

Bird life cycles

A female bird lays eggs with hard shells. The eggs are **fertilized** inside her body. Most birds build nests to provide safe places to lay their eggs and raise their young. The eggs must be kept warm if they are to develop properly and hatch into healthy chicks. This is called the **incubation period**. One parent, usually the female, sits on the eggs, holding them against the **brood patch** on its breast. Some eggs take about ten days to hatch, others as long as two months. Birds are caring parents. They stay with their chicks and bring them food until the chicks have learned to fly and can find food for themselves.

Birds' eggs

A bird's egg contains everything a young bird needs to survive and grow. Its hard shell gives protection but is covered with tiny holes to let oxygen in. The white of the egg, or **albumen**, contains water for the young bird. The **yolk** is its food supply. When the chick is fully developed, it cracks the shell open with its bony egg-tooth and struggles out.

A male emperor penguin **incubating** its egg between its feet.

Penguin parents

Emperor penguins nest on the Antarctic ice in temperatures of -62°C. The female lays a single egg, then swims off to sea to feed. The male cradles the egg in the warm space between his feet and his feathered belly, where it is protected by a flap of skin. Then he spends about three months in the freezing cold, without eating and hardly moving, until the egg hatches. Then the female returns to feed the chick.

Growing up

Different types of birds mature at different rates. Some young birds, such as goslings and ducklings, leave the nest almost immediately, although they still stay close to their parents. Others, such as pigeons and woodpeckers, are blind and helpless. Their parents have to feed them constantly. The same is true of learning to fly. A baby mallee fowl can fly within a day of hatching from its egg, whereas it takes a wandering albatross about nine months to make its first flight from its nest. Up until the time it takes its first flight it relies totally on its parents for food and protection.

An albatross on its nest with its chick.

Did you know?
In the wild, most small birds only live for about two to five years. Larger birds live for longer, up to 20 or 30 years. But most wild birds do not die of old age. Millions are killed by **predators**, such as foxes and rats, or by cars. Others starve when food is scarce, or die from disease. Altogether, about three-quarters die before they are six months old. The longest-lived birds are thought to be wandering albatrosses, which may live for about 80 years.

Mammal life cycles

Mammals are the group of animals to which human beings belong. They range in size from huge whales and elephants to tiny shrews and bats. Mammals reproduce **sexually** and are the only animals that produce milk to suckle their young. They feed and care for their young until they are old enough to fend for themselves. Most mammals give birth to live young that develop inside their mothers' bodies, after female egg cells have been **fertilized** by male **sperm**. But two special types of mammals, the **monotremes** and the **marsupials**, have more unusual life cycles.

Egg-laying mammals

Monotremes are very unusual mammals. There are three **species** – the duck-billed platypus, the long-beaked echidna and the short-beaked echidna. The echidnas are also known as spiny anteaters. Monotremes are the only mammals that lay eggs. The platypus lays two soft, leathery eggs in a nest in a riverbank burrow. An echidna lays a single egg, which it carries in a small pouch underneath its body. When the egg hatches, the baby feeds on its mother's milk. The milk oozes on to the mother's fur and the young animal laps it up.

A short-beaked echidna.

Kangaroo life cycle

Marsupials are mammals with pouches, such as koalas, kangaroos and opossums. The females have pocket-like pouches on their stomachs. Like other marsupials, a new-born kangaroo, or joey, is tiny, blind and helpless. It has to develop inside its mother's pouch before it can fend for itself. Here you can follow a kangaroo's life cycle.

1. At birth, the baby kangaroo is only about two centimetres long. It crawls up its mother's fur and into her pouch.

2. Inside the pouch, it attaches itself to one of her teats. It starts to drink its mother's milk and to grow.

3. The joey begins to look more like a kangaroo. After about six months, it leaves the pouch for the first time but soon hops back inside.

4. When it is about nine months old, it leaves the pouch for good. By this time, another joey may already be suckling inside. A kangaroo lives for 15 – 20 years.

Did you know?

The Virginia opossum, a marsupial from North America, has the shortest pregnancy of any mammal. It lasts for a maximum of thirteen days and can be as short as eight days. The baby mammal spends another four to five weeks developing inside its mother's pouch. The opossum also has the most young, with about 20 babies in a litter.

Placental mammals

Apart from **monotremes** and **marsupials**, all other mammals are called **placental** mammals. Their young grow and develop inside the mothers' bodies until they are fully formed. A baby placental mammal is born looking like a smaller version of its parents. **Fertilization** takes place internally. Then the baby develops inside its mother's uterus, or womb. The baby gets oxygen and

nourishment from its mother, through a spongy layer of cells called the placenta. In the placenta, the mother's blood supply lies close to that of the baby. Food and oxygen pass from the mother's blood into the baby's blood, and waste products pass the other way.

A mare (female horse) suckling its foal on milk.

Blue whale babies

Unlike those of most mammals, sea mammal babies are born tail first. Sea mammals, such as whales and dolphins, must come to the surface to breathe air to stay alive. Being born tail first stops them from drowning as they are being born. The babies are pushed to the surface by their mother to take their first breath.

Blue whales have the largest babies of any mammal. At birth, a blue whale calf is already six to eight metres long and weighs two to three tonnes. It drinks 200 litres (a small bathtub-full) of its mother's milk a day. By the time it is weaned, at seven months old, it can weigh up to 20 tonnes. Blue whales can live for up to 65 years.

Batty nurseries

Each year, millions of free-tailed bats fly from Mexico to Texas, USA, to have their young. They raise them inside cave nurseries where they are warm and safe from **predators**. The caves are dark and very crowded. One of them, Bracken Cave, contains some ten million baby bats. At night, the females leave the cave to search for food. When they return, they are able to find their own baby in the crowd, by recognizing its particular call and smell.

Baby faces

All mammals look after their young but the length of care varies from a few weeks in mice to several years in apes. A baby mammal's appearance often shows that it needs to be looked after. A baby orang-utan, for example, is small, with big eyes and jerky movements. This sends a message to adult orang-utans that it needs to be cared for.

An orang-utan baby with its mother.

Did you know?

The shortest-lived mammal is the tiny shrew. It only lives for 12–18 months in the wild. It is born one year, breeds the next, then dies. The elephant has the longest lifespan (other than humans). The oldest on record was an elephant called Raja, who died in captivity at the age of 82. In the wild, many Asian elephants live to be 55 – 70 years old.

Human life cycles

Like whales, orang-utans and bats, human beings are **placental** mammals. A human baby develops inside its mother until it is ready to be born. Then its mother feeds it on milk and takes care of it. Humans care for their young for longer than any other mammals.

How a baby grows

Over nine months, the **fertilized** cell grows and develops into a tiny human being. Here you can follow a baby's life cycle from the first month to when it is ready to be born.

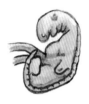
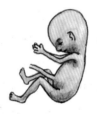

Month 1 – The baby's heart begins to beat.

Month 2 – The baby has tiny hands and feet.

Month 3 – The baby is fully formed.

Month 4 – The baby grows hair, eyebrows, eyelashes, toenails and fingernails.

Month 5 – The baby grows quickly, though its head is still much bigger than its body.

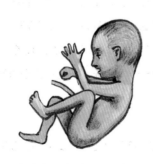

Month 6 – The baby has a set pattern of sleeping and waking.

Month 7 – The baby moves about in the womb. Its lungs are working.

Month 8 – The baby starts to suck its thumb, ready to suck its mother's milk.

Month 9 – The baby turns head down. It is ready to be born.

28

A baby begins

Like every other person, you started life as a tiny cell. This formed when a **sperm** cell from your father joined with an **ovum** cell from your mother. The fertilized cell began to divide until it formed a ball of cells. Then it embedded itself in the lining of your mother's uterus, or womb, where you received food and oxygen through the placenta.

Growing up

In the first two years of life, you grow very quickly. At 18 months old, a girl is almost half of her adult height. A boy reaches this stage at about two years old. You then grow steadily until you are about ten, when you shoot up again. Between the ages of 11 and 13, your body starts to change into an adult. This is called **puberty**. Girls begin to grow breasts and have **periods**. Boys grow hair on their bodies and their voices 'break' and become deeper. Your body stops growing when you are about 20 years old, though it carries on changing as you get older.

Growing old

At about 60 to 70 years old, people begin to show more signs of ageing. It takes longer for the wear and tear on their bodies to be repaired. Their skin loses its elastic quality and becomes wrinkled. Their hair may turn grey or white as it loses its colouring **pigment**. People also shrink as they grow older because the discs of cartilage between their backbones shrink and their spines become shorter. Today, many people live to 80 or 90 because of healthier lifestyles.

Conclusion

Life cycles are often linked to the seasons. Spring is a time when many plants start to bloom and many animals have their young. In winter, nature is barren and bare. But nature's life cycles are going on around us, all the time. Reproduction is a part of all these life cycles and one of the key life processes of all living things. It is how new life is created so that a new cycle can begin.

Glossary

abdomen the back part of an insect's or arachnid's body

albumen the white of an egg

amphibians animals such as frogs, toads and newts, that live both in and out of water

annuals plants which only live for a year. In that time, they grow, produce their flowers and die.

arachnids the group of animals which includes spiders, scorpions, ticks and mites – they all have eight legs

asexual a form of reproduction that does not involve sex and in which only one parent is needed. The parent splits in two, or buds or splits off, to produce a new individual.

brood patch a bare patch of skin on a bird's breast for keeping the bird's eggs warm during incubation

chlorophyll a green pigment (colouring) found inside plant cells. It absorbs energy from sunlight for use in photosynthesis.

chrysalis the hard outer case protecting a pupa

cotyledon the seed leaf where food for the germinating plant is stored

fertile able to reproduce

fertilization, fertilize the joining together of a male and female sex cell (gametes) to produce a new living thing

fronds the leaves of ferns

fungi one kingdom of living things which includes toadstools, mushrooms and moulds

gametes the individual male or female sex cells

genetic to do with genes. Genes are chemical codes which say what a living thing is and what it looks like.

germinate, germination the early growth of a seed into a plant

gills 1) fine ridges on the underside of a mushroom or toadstool's cap on which spores grow
2) feathery organs which fish use for breathing oxygen in water

glucose a simple sugar – plants store food as glucose

habitat a particular area in which certain plants and animals live

incubation period the length of time an animal incubates its eggs

incubating keeping eggs warm until the young hatch out

iodine a type of chemical

kingdom in scientific classification, the largest group of living things. There are five kingdoms including plants, animals and fungi.

larvae a stage in the life cycle of some animals. Larvae are young forms that look very different from the adults.

marsupials mammals whose young develop in pouches on the female's body and suckle milk

metamorphosis the series of changes insects go through as they change from eggs into adults

monotremes mammals which lay eggs and then feed their young on milk after they hatch

moult some animals moult, or shed, their skins in order to grow

nectar a sweet, sugary liquid made inside a flower

nuclei the plural of nucleus. The nucleus is a round structure inside a cell. It is the cell's control centre, regulating everything that happens inside the cell.

nymphs young insect forms that look very much like adults

ovule a female sex cell of a plant

ovum the special sex cell (gamete) made by a female animal

parasites plants or animals which live on or in other plants or animals and get all their food from them

perennials plants which live for many years but die down at the end of each season and shoot up at the start of the next

periods a small amount of blood which comes from a woman's body once a month if she releases an egg and the egg is not fertilized

photosynthesis the process by which green plants make food from carbon dioxide and water, using energy from sunlight absorbed by their chlorophyll

pigment a natural colouring or dye

placental mammals who give birth to live young and then suckle them on milk

pollen tiny grains which are the male sex cells of flowering plants

pollination the transfer of pollen from a male flower to a female flower or from the male part of a flower to the female part

predators animals which hunt and kill other animals for food

puberty a time in a boy or girl's life when their bodies change from being a child to being an adult

pupae a stage in the life cycle of some insects. Inside the pupa a larva develops into an adult.

reptiles animals such as snakes, turtles, crocodiles and lizards

sexual a form of reproduction which needs two parents, one male and one female. Each makes sex cells which must join together to create a new individual.

spawn another name for the eggs of fish, frogs and some other animals. To spawn also means to lay eggs.

species a set of organisms (living things) which are grouped together because they have similar features and can breed with each other

sperm the special sex cells (gamete) made by a male animal

sporangia a structure in which spores are produced in ferns

spores microscopic reproductive cells produced by fungi and some plants like ferns

yolk the yellow part of an egg

zygote the cell which is made when two sex cells (gametes) join together – the beginning of new life

Index